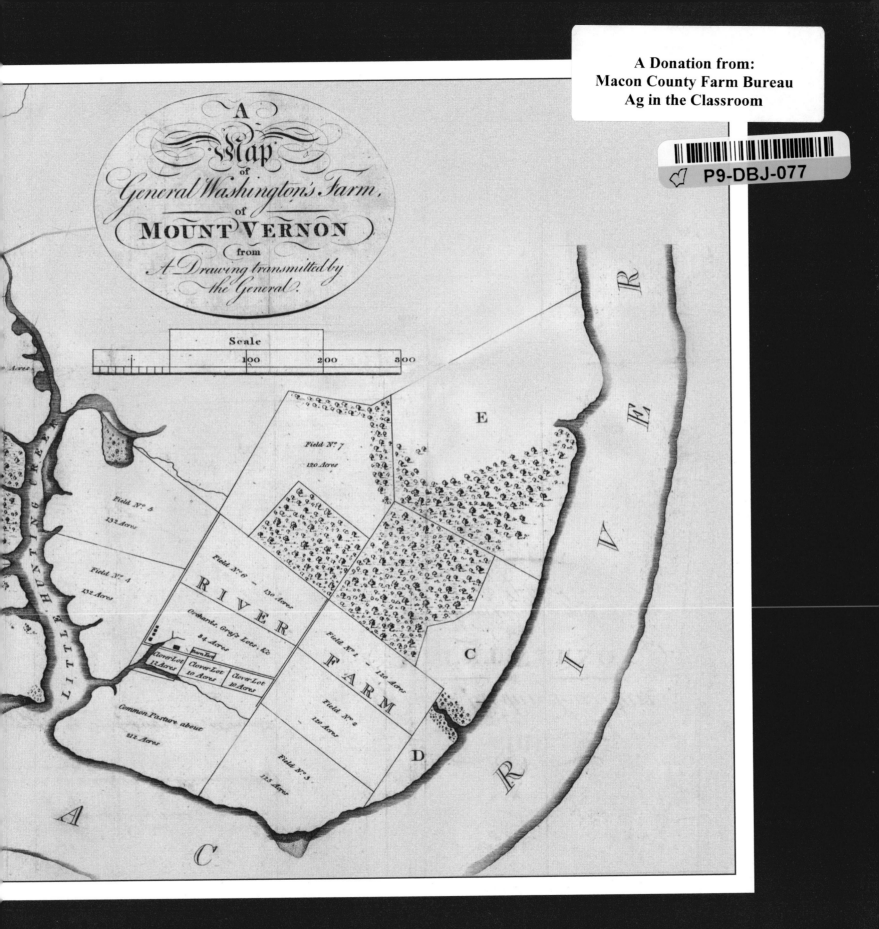

A Map of General Washington's Farm, of MOUNT VERNON from A Drawing transmitted by the General.

Scale
100    200    300

Field Nº 7
120 Acres

Field Nº 5
132 Acres

Field Nº 4
132 Acres

Field Nº 6 — 130 Acres

Orchards, Grass Lots, &c
54 Acres

Clover Lot
12 Acres

Clover Lot
10 Acres

Clover Lot
10 Acres

Common Pasture about
212 Acres

RIVER FARM

Field Nº 1 — 120 Acres

Field Nº 2
130 Acres

Field Nº 3
125 Acres

LITTLE HUNTINGING CREEK

E

C

D

A

C

R    I    V    E    R

# Farmer George

## Plants a Nation

Peggy Thomas
Paintings by Layne Johnson

CALKINS CREEK
AN IMPRINT OF HIGHLIGHTS
*Honesdale, Pennsylvania*

*In memory of my father, Howard Facklam, who, I imagine, has already talked to George about fertilizer, seeds, and trees*
PT

*To my mother—who taught me what* Gee and Haw *mean*
LJ

**Acknowledgments**

I would like to thank the helpful staff at Mount Vernon Estate & Gardens, especially research specialist Mary V. Thompson, for reading the manuscript and providing welcome comments and corrections, and librarian Barbara McMillan. A special thanks to my editor, Carolyn P. Yoder, for her patience through the long revision process.

All quotations are reprinted with permission from John C. Fitzpatrick's *The Writings of George Washington from the Original Manuscript Sources, 1745–1799* and *The Diaries of George Washington*, edited by Donald Jackson and Dorothy Twohig, as part of the George Washington Papers at the Library of Congress. —*PT*

Many thanks to Mary V. Thompson, Jennifer Lane, and the pioneer farm folks at Mount Vernon Estate & Gardens. —*LJ*

Cover and interior design by CPorter Designs

Endsheets: A map of George Washington's farm of Mount Vernon from a drawing transmitted by the General—Library of Congress, Geography and Map Division

Calkins Creek
An Imprint of Highlights
815 Church Street
Honesdale, Pennsylvania 18431
Printed in China

**Library of Congress Cataloging-in-Publication Data**

Thomas, Peggy.
  Farmer George plants a nation / Peggy Thomas ; illustrations by Layne Johnson. — 1st ed.
     p. cm.
  Includes bibliographical references.
  ISBN: 978-1-59078-460-0 (hc) • ISBN: 978-1-62091-029-0 (pb)
  1. Washington, George, 1732-1799—Juvenile literature.
  2. Washington, George, 1732-1799—Homes and haunts—Juvenile literature. 3. Family farms—Virginia—Mount Vernon (Estate)—History—Juvenile literature. 4. Mount Vernon (Va : Estate)—History—Juvenile literature. I. Johnson, Layne. II. Title.

E312.5.T54 2008
973.4'1092—dc22
[B]
2007018449

First edition
The text of this book is set in Cushing.
The illustrations are done in oils on canvas.
10 9 8 7 6 5

George Washington dug his hand into the newly tilled earth and let the hard, dry clay crumble through his long fingers.

_S_tanding a head taller than his field hands, George scanned the distant landscape, imagining how much tobacco, corn, and wheat it would produce. He had always loved Mount Vernon, even before his half brother Lawrence named the estate after Admiral Edward Vernon, a great British naval officer. George remembered living there as a boy, running after chickens and following Lawrence as he inspected the fields.

In 1759, at the age of twenty-seven, George was master of the estate. He had just returned home from four years of fighting in the French and Indian War. Being commander in chief of Virginia's troops was difficult, but young George learned to lead and make decisions with confidence. Now that he was home, he had his lovely wife, Martha, and two stepchildren to care for and a busy plantation to run.

How would this poor soil grow the crops he needed to feed his family and slaves, and earn money at market, too? George had learned a lot watching Lawrence, but he needed to know more to make his plantation successful.

*S*o he penned a letter to England, ordering the best books on agriculture, including Batty Langley's *New Principles of Gardening*. These books would not have all the answers George needed. They were based on what worked for British farmers. George would need to see for himself which seeds would grow well in Mount Vernon's hard clay soil and warm Virginia climate.

ne blustery day in March, George watched as the field hands planted crops. One guided a wheeled plow, turning over clods of dirt. A second slave walked behind, scattering handfuls of barley seed. A third field hand covered the seeds with soil using a sharp harrow. There had to be a better way, George thought.

Later, he wrote in his diary:

*Spent the greatest part of the day in making a new plow of my own Invention.* (1760)

For one of his new plows, he found a barrel and punched holes slightly bigger than a seed into the side. Then he fastened the barrel to the top of the plow. Now as the field hand guided the plow forward, the barrel turned as the plow cut the earth. Seeds dropped out of the barrel's small holes, tumbled down a chute, and fell into the tilled ground in neat rows. A harrow attached to the back of the plow covered the seeds with soil. George was delighted. His new plow did three jobs at once, saving time and energy.

The new plow helped his field hands plant faster, but nothing helped the tired soil recover from years of planting tobacco. Tobacco was a harsh crop that soaked up all of the soil's nutrients. Other plantation owners planted tobacco in the same field year after year until the soil was too weak to nurture more seeds. Then they abandoned the field, moved to a new plot, and started all over again.

Such a waste, George thought. Instead, he rotated the crops he grew within a single field and experimented with different fertilizers.

He tested soil and manure in his little garden nestled between the salt house and the upper garden wall. He'd roll up his sleeves and drill holes in the soil, precisely measuring the distances between them. Rather than use a proper label, George marked each row with a notched stick and kept track in his diary of what each marking meant.

He'd mix different composts and soils in a large wooden box that was divided into sections.

*Mix'd my Composts in a box with ten Apartments in the following manner . . .* (1760)

He would toss horse manure in one part, cow manure in the second, and sheep manure in another. Then he would plant the same number of seeds in each section. Each day he would check on his experiment and write down what he saw. Which sprouts broke the soil first? How healthy did they look, and how fast did they grow? The best fertilizers were then used in the big fields.

George believed that "every experiment is a treasure," and he enjoyed sharing the results of his experiments with guests and neighbors who visited. They had the same problems.

His dinner guests also complained about how expensive it was to ship their tobacco to England. They groaned about the new taxes they were forced to pay to the King of England—a tax on sugar, a tax on tea, on glass, paint, and lead. There was even a special stamp required for newspapers and documents. It seemed unfair for the colonists to pay such high taxes when they had no voice in the British government. George agreed.

Each year he planted less and less tobacco so he did not have to ship it to England. Instead he grew more and more wheat to sell to other colonists; potatoes, turnips, and other vegetables to feed his household; and flax to make cloth. Soon Mount Vernon was like a little village.

14

*S*triding down the north lane, George could hear the whir of spinning wheels and the thwack of the looms as slaves and hired weavers wove cloth for blankets and clothing. *Tap, tap, tap,* sounded the shoemaker's hammer, and loud clanging from the blacksmith's anvil echoed up from the stables. Nothing was purchased from England that could be made at Mount Vernon. As George made Mount Vernon less dependent on English goods, the colonists' grumblings grew louder. It was time for the colonies to break away from England, too.

Although George loved Mount Vernon, too many people were calling for him to leave home to lead the colonies as commander in chief of the Continental Army. He could not refuse. In June 1775, General George Washington rode off to train his troops to fight the British. When he left, George thought, as all the soldiers did, that he would be home by Christmas. But he would not live at Mount Vernon again for more than eight years.

No matter where he was, George's thoughts were never far from home. When he was huddled in a drafty tent overlooking a battlefield, or at a desk in a crowded inn, General George found time to write lengthy letters to his farm managers back home. The longest was sixteen pages!

Days before leading rows of soldiers into battle, he eased his mind by imagining where to plant rows of fruit trees. He wrote to his cousin Lund of his plans.

*I mean to have groves of Trees at each end of the dwelling House . . . to range in a line from the South East Corner to Colo. Fairfax's . . .* (1776)

And from his dismal makeshift headquarters in New Windsor, New York, he could imagine a brighter future at home.

*How many Lambs have you had this Spring? How many Colts are you like to have? . . . An acct. of these things would be satisfactory to me . . . as I have these kind of improvements very much at heart.* (1781)

Finally, on Christmas Eve 1783, a victorious George Washington trotted up the road to Mount Vernon. He had won the war and now looked forward to living as a simple farmer again.

But his farms looked shabby and his fields looked tired. He tried new mixes of fertilizer: plaster of Paris, black muck from the swamp, and fish heads. He even looked into pulling mud from the bottom of the Potomac River with a new machine called "the Hippopotamus."

George may have missed being a general, though, for he plotted and planted trees as if they were soldiers on a battlefield. Redbud and dogwood trees guarded the house. Magnolias and black locusts shielded the servants' quarters, and weeping willows and oaks stood sentinel along the roads.

And wherever he traveled, he brought back a pocketful of seeds or nuts to experiment with. Each day he would record his work in his diary.

 *Planted & Sowed . . . Six buck eye nuts, brought with me from the Mouth of Cheat River . . . [and] Six acorns, which I brought with me from the South Branch.* (1785)

21

After the war, he did not have as much time to plant or experiment. He was a hero. People wanted to meet him, shake his hand, and ask his advice. Guests arrived almost every day. Many brought gifts. His friends knew just what he liked.

*I will receive with great pleasure and gratitude the seeds of any trees or shrubs wch. are not natives of this country . . .* (1786)

But the strangest gift *clip-clopped* up to the steps of Mount Vernon on December 5, 1785. It was a prized male donkey from King Charles III of Spain. Its handler, Pedro Tellez, had walked the donkey all the way from Boston, where they landed after a long trip across the Atlantic Ocean. George was so pleased with the large and powerful animal that he called it Royal Gift.

A year later his friend the Marquis de Lafayette of France sent him two female donkeys and another male donkey, called Knight of Malta. Farmer George bred the male donkeys with female horses to create some of the finest American mules. He believed that every farmer should use mules because they were stronger than horses and more agile than oxen. Soon many American farmers would have one.

Farmer George spread the news about the powerful mules and shared all he learned about crops and fertilizers with other farmers. He believed that all of his experiments and each improvement he made at Mount Vernon would benefit everyone. America needed many successful farmers in order to grow into a successful nation.

 *For, in the present State of America, our welfare and prosperity depend upon the cultivation of our lands and turning the produce of them to the best advantage.* (1788)

23

24

Even though he was no longer an army general, he was still leading the way by his actions and his words. In 1789 his leadership was made official again. George Washington was elected the first president of the United States of America.

On April 16, 1789, he stepped into his carriage and took one last look at his quiet countryside home.

*About ten o'clock I bade adieu to Mount Vernon . . .* (1789)

Days later he arrived in the bustling new capital, New York City, to take the oath of office and invent the job of president. He chose judges, picked cabinet members, and approved laws. He visited each new state, talking to governors, mayors, and, of course, farmers to share what he knew and learn about their problems.

At the same time he was building a new government, President George Washington took time to think about buildings on his farms. From his presidential desk, he designed a barn like no other. It had sixteen sides and was two stories tall. He designed it so his workers could tread wheat inside during bad weather.

When wheat was harvested, the grains had to be separated from the stalks by treading, or walking, on it. The workers would usually do this outside on the ground in good weather or bad. This bothered George.

When he sent plans for the construction of the treading barn to his farm manager at Mount Vernon, he ordered his brickmakers to fashion 30,820 bricks. He chose to build the barn on the side of a hill so that horses could be led in and out on an earthen ramp. Workers would no longer tread the wheat; horses would. The horses would trot in a circle on the upper level. Instead of a solid wood floor, George designed a floor with sturdy slats placed one and a half inches apart. It was safe enough for the horses and allowed the small grains of wheat to fall through the cracks to the floor below. There, workers shoveled the grain and placed it in bags for grinding.

*P*resident George thought a lot about manure, too. He shared his thoughts with other Founding Fathers, including Thomas Jefferson.

*A Mr. Bartrand, a famous Agriculturalist . . . put into my hands a few days ago several papers . . . on the Subject of Manuring and vegitation. . . . Nothing, is more wanting in this Country, than a thorough knowledge of the first.* (April 1794)

His composting experiments grew larger when he designed a building called a stercorary, or dung house. Located by the stables, it was long and narrow and had open sides to allow air and odor to flow in and out. He told his farm manager:

*. . . let others rake, and scrape up all the trash, of every sort and kind about the houses, and in holes and corners, and throw it (all I mean that will make dung) into the Stercorary . . .* (1796)

There the waste was left to decompose before it was spread on the fields.

George was president for eight years and defined what it meant to hold that office. But in 1797, it was time for George to go home. No longer general, no longer president, he was just Farmer George.

 *Worn out in a manner by the toils of my past labour, I am again seated under my Vine and Fig tree . . .* (1798)

He counted and inspected his livestock and still kept his eye on the army. He continued to give advice to other farmers and occasionally gave advice to the new president. He managed his farms, puttered in his little garden, and wrote in his diary.

On December 12, 1799, two days before he died, he noted that it was wet, cold, and snowy. But George did what all good farmers do: he rode out to inspect his fields. It would be the last time.

$\mathcal{G}$eorge once wrote,

*I hope, some day or another, we shall become a storehouse and granary for the world.* (1788)

And because of George Washington, we are.

He planted the seed of freedom on the battlefield, and with his ingenuity as a farmer and his leadership as the nation's first president, the United States grew into a world leader in farming. Until the end—general, president, farmer—George Washington led his country by example.

*Liberty, when it begins to take root, is a plant of rapid growth.* (1788)

# Timeline

**1732** — George Washington is born on February 22

**1743** — Father, Augustine, dies. George Washington spends time with half brother Lawrence at Mount Vernon

**1748** — Goes on a surveying expedition in the Shenandoah Valley

**1749** — Becomes a professional surveyor

**1752** — Lawrence Washington dies

**1754** — Fights in the French and Indian War. Leases Mount Vernon from Lawrence's widow

**1756** — Orders first books about agriculture

**1758** — Returns home to Mount Vernon

**1759** — Marries Martha Custis on January 6. Orders Batty Langley's gardening book

**1760** — Invents a new plow design

**1761** — Inherits Mount Vernon when Lawrence's widow dies

**1766** — Stops growing tobacco as the main cash crop

**1767** — Creates a cloth-making industry at Mount Vernon

**1775** — Becomes commander in chief of the Continental Army and fights the British in the American Revolution

**1783** — Returns home as a retired general

**1785** — Receives Royal Gift from the King of Spain

**1786** — Begins correspondence with Arthur Young, a leading farmer in England

**1787** — Builds the stercorary; serves as president of the Constitutional Convention

**1789** — Elected the first president of the United States

**1792** — Designs and begins to build sixteen-sided barn (completed in 1794)

**1797** — Returns home to Mount Vernon after eight years as president

**1799** — Dies December 14

# George at Mount Vernon

George Washington is most famous for his role as a general in the American Revolution and as the first president of the United States. But he was a general only for eight and a half years and held the office of president for eight years. Most of his time was spent on his land at Mount Vernon, overlooking the Potomac River.

When he leased Mount Vernon in 1754, it covered about two thousand acres. But under his leadership, the estate grew to more than eight thousand acres and was divided into five different farms: Dogue Run, Union Farm, Muddy Hole, River Farm, and Mansion House Farm, where George and Martha's "Home House" still stands.

George tackled every problem with a courageous spirit and paid close attention to detail. He fought for what he believed in, and was not afraid to try new ideas and experiment with unusual tools. Over his lifetime he renovated the mansion, designed new buildings, changed the way his farms made money, and experimented with more than sixty kinds of field crops and countless more shrubs, vegetables, flowering plants, and trees.

Yes, George loved trees. It was a myth, written after his death, that George chopped down a cherry tree in his youth. In reality, he might have planted more trees than he ever cut down.

Today you can visit Mount Vernon and sit under some of the trees that George planted more than two hundred years ago. Close your eyes, and when you hear the mules braying in their stalls and smell the sweet fragrance of magnolia, you can just imagine Farmer George off in the distance, riding home.

# George's Thoughts on Slavery

Like most owners of large estates in the 1700s, George relied on slaves to carry out the work on his farms. At the time of his death in 1799, more than three hundred slaves lived and worked at Mount Vernon. They planted, hoed, and harvested the crops, built his barns, cooked his food, washed his clothes, and drew his bath.

Because he had switched from growing labor-intensive tobacco to wheat, which required less work, George actually had more workers than he needed. But George would not sell his slaves. He hated the thought of breaking up families.

*. . . it is . . . against my inclination . . . to hurt the feelings of those unhappy people by a separation of man and wife, or of families.* (1786)

Although slaves were a normal and accepted part of life in the South during the American Revolution, George came to believe that slavery was wrong.

*I never mean . . . to possess another slave by purchase; it being among my first wishes to see some plan adopted, by which slavery in this country may be abolished by slow, sure, and imperceptible degrees.* (1786)

But George kept his concerns to himself. He was afraid that slaveholders in other parts of the country would leave the union if he pushed for the end of slavery. More than anything else, George wanted to preserve the new fragile nation he fought so hard to create. Although George did not promote abolishing slavery publicly, he did take steps as a private slave owner to free his slaves upon his death. He was the only slave-owning president to do so.

# Learn More About Farmer George at Mount Vernon

## Books

Bial, Raymond. *Where Washington Walked.* New York: Walker and Co., 2004.

Collier, James Lincoln. *The George Washington You Never Knew.* New York: Children's Press, 2003.

Reef, Catherine. *Mount Vernon.* New York: Dillon Press, 1992.

Santella, Andrew. *Mount Vernon.* Minneapolis: Compass Point Books, 2005.

Yoder, Carolyn, ed. *George Washington the Writer: A Treasury of Letters, Diaries, and Public Documents.* Honesdale, PA: Boyds Mills Press, 2003.

## Website*

George Washington's Mount Vernon Estate & Gardens. www.mountvernon.org. Take a virtual tour of the mansion, and learn about George Washington as a pioneer farmer.

*Active at the time of publication

## Take a Trip

The best way to get to know George Washington as a farmer is to visit Mount Vernon Estate & Gardens. Explore the Ford Orientation Center and Donald W. Reynolds Museum and Education Center that is tucked below the fields of grazing sheep, and tour George and Martha's mansion home. Stroll through his little garden, and step back in time to the bustle of a working eighteenth-century farm.

The Mount Vernon Estate is located sixteen miles south of Washington, D.C., at 3200 Mount Vernon Memorial Highway, Mount Vernon, Virginia 22121.

39

# Bibliography

## Books

Andrist, Ralph K. *George Washington: A Biography in His Own Words.* 2 vols. New York: Newsweek, 1972.

*Colonial Gardens: The Landscape Architecture of George Washington's Time.* Washington, DC: U.S. George Washington Bicentennial Commission, 1932.

Dies, Edward Jerome. *Titans of the Soil: Great Builders of Agriculture.* Westport, CT: Greenwood Press, 1976.

Ford, Paul Leicester. *The True George Washington.* Philadelphia: J. B. Lippincott, 1896.

Fusonie, Alan, and Donna Jean Fusonie. *George Washington: Pioneer Farmer.* Mount Vernon, VA: Mount Vernon Ladies' Association, 1998.

Greenberg, Allan. *George Washington, Architect.* London: Andreas Papadakis Publisher, 1999.

Griswold, Mac. *Washington's Gardens at Mount Vernon: Landscape of the Inner Man.* Boston: Houghton Mifflin, 1999.

Meyer, Jeffrey G. *America's Famous and Historic Trees: From George Washington's Tulip Poplar to Elvis Presley's Pin Oak.* Boston: Houghton Mifflin, 2001.

*Mount Vernon: An Illustrated Handbook.* Mount Vernon, VA: The Mount Vernon Ladies' Association, 1974.

Padover, Saul K., ed. *The Washington Papers: Basic Selections from the Public and Private Writings of George Washington.* New York: Harper and Brothers, 1955.

Twohig, Dorothy, ed. *George Washington Diaries: An Abridgment.* Charlottesville, VA: University Press of Virginia, 1999.

## Articles

Abbot, W. W. "George Washington in Retirement." The Lowell Lecture Series, The Museum of Our National Heritage, Lexington, Massachusetts, December 5, 1999. The Papers of George Washington. www.gwpapers.virginia.edu/articles/abbot_1.html.

Boule, John Richard, II. "Washington—Engineer and Engineer Advocate." *Engineer: The Professional Bulletin of Army Engineers,* January–March 2003, 51–55.

Chase, Philander D. "Thoughts of Home: General Washington Kept a Picture of Mount Vernon in His Mind's Eye During the Revolutionary War." 1995. The Papers of George Washington. www.gwpapers.virginia.edu/articles/chase.html.

Kelleher, David. "From Malta to Washington: A Gift Fit for a President." *The Malta Independent,* April 30, 2000.

Pogue, Dennis J. "America's First Composter." *Urban Agriculture Notes,* February 1997.

Pogue, Dennis J. "George Washington and the Politics of Slavery." *Historic Alexandria Quarterly,* Spring–Summer 2003.

## Databases and Websites*

Fitzpatrick, John Clement. *The Writings of George Washington from the Original Manuscript Sources.* Washington, DC: U.S. Government Print Office, 1931–1944. http://etext.lib.virginia.edu/washington/fitzpatrick.

George Washington Papers at the Library of Congress, 1741–1799. www.memory.loc.gov/ammem/gwhtml/gwhome.html.

George Washington's Mount Vernon Estate & Gardens. www.mountvernon.org.

*Active at the time of publication

### Artist's Note

To create art for this book, I started with one of the best sources, George himself. George Washington's diaries contain a treasure of information about George's life, his opinions, and his thoughts on farming. But to gain real insight, I visited George Washington's home—Mount Vernon. As I stood on the piazza of the Virginia mansion, I could almost feel George beside me, looking out over the Potomac. Watching the gentle waters, George might have been contemplating what crops to rotate, how he could improve his barrel seeder, or what trees he would plant down the north lane. With the help of Mount Vernon experts Mary Thompson and Jennifer Lane, I was able to gain a fresh insight into George's farming world. I watched horses tread wheat in the restored treading barn, feeling the timbers shake as the horses stomped their hooves over the unthreshed grain. Standing in George's study, I could almost see George sitting at his desk, planning his next project. Anyone can visit Mount Vernon and experience this living history—seeing the beautifully restored mansion the way George and Martha knew it in 1799. I learned that with George Washington's leadership, innovation, and perseverance, George's agricultural vision for the country became a reality. As everyone knows, George Washington was a Founding Father, but his legacy as a founding farmer should not be forgotten. —*LJ*

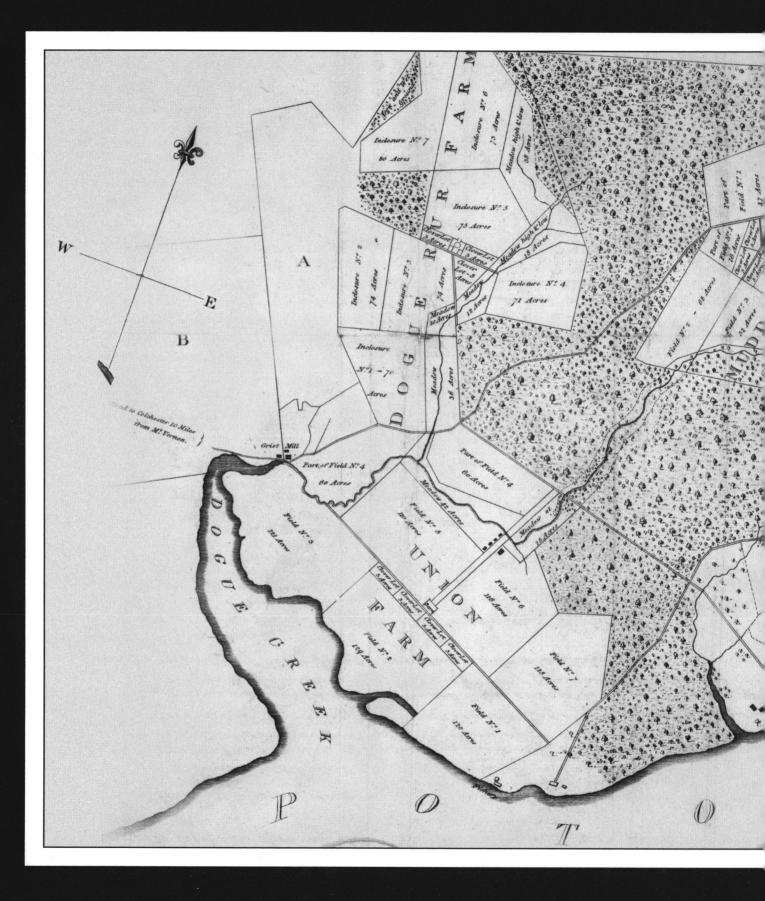